FORWARD

Ashes to ashes, dust to dust. This is what happens to your body, but your soul goes on forever!

* * *

I can only tell you what I know, and what I've learned from the other side. I learn more from them every day, and every time I connect then to their loved ones here. There is a wealth of knowledge on the other side that is still untapped. I feel we've barely scratched the surface on what we can learn from our loved ones and guides on the other side. My goal with this book is to try and explain some of the things I've learned from the other side, and to help those of you that want to awaken, and tap into your own abilities. Some of the things I've learned can be a little difficult to grasp, and may not be complete, because they give me what I need to know when I need to know it. That's kind of how it works. Every day I learn something else new!

CONTENTS

A NIGHT ON THE OTHER SIDE

Insights and conversations from "heaven"

June Edward
"The
Massachusetts
Medium"

I dedicate this book to my love of many lifetimes, my twin flame Rob. He was the catalyst for me in this life time to facilitate my awakening, and truly bring fourth my gifts. Without him I would still be in darkness, he truly made me a better person.

HOW I BECAME A PSYCHIC MEDIUM

I am a Psychic Medium. According to my astrological chart, I was definitely born this way. My first experience that I can remember was about the age of three years old. I can remember my parents having to use a sunporch as a bedroom, for me and my younger sister, since there were eight children in the family, and not enough bedrooms. My parent's bedroom was through the living room and down the hall, but would have been up against one wall of the room I was sleeping in. I remember that the curtains were very scary looking to me as a small child. They were heavy drapes with green leaves, but I kept seeing faces in them when I looked at them. One night I was asleep, and it was just about dawn. I thought I heard my father calling my name. I got out of bed and ran into their room, only to find them fast asleep. I went back to bed, and heard it again. I was so scared I pulled the covers over my head. My sister, about two at the time, was also fast asleep across the room. After I pulled the covers over my head, I saw a dark black shadow come over my bed and lean over me. I could see it through the covers. I was so scared I couldn't even scream. I closed my eyes, and waited until it was gone. This happened one more time, and then I refused to sleep in the bed anymore. I would let my parents put me to bed, and as soon as it was quiet, I would move to the couch in the living room.

As I got older, I just knew things before they were going to happen. If I mentioned it to my friends, they started to act strange towards me. It made me extremely nervous, and self-conscience. So much that I was developing a nervous twitch and started to stutter! I stopped telling people what I knew.

My parents split up when I was around ten years old. The youngest five of us ended up with my father, because he apparently kidnapped us! My mother knew where we were, but wasn't allowed to see us. We were also told that she was crazy, and didn't want us. The reality of it was, my mother didn't work, and figured my father would go to jail, and she wouldn't have any way to support us. In that case, she felt we would end up in foster care, so she stayed away as she was told. Years later I reconnected with my mother, and found out she was far from crazy, but was also a Medium!

My job at the time as a child of ten years old was to do the dishes every day for all of us. My next oldest sister at the time would do the cooking. I would usually do them all in the late afternoon around four or five o'clock, when I was the only one in the house, and everyone else was outside playing or spending time with friends.

There was always a woman that would stand next to the sink with me, and keep me company talking while I did the dishes. She never scared me, she was about fifty year's old, and seemed very kind. We would just talk about random things, nothing really memorable; I just enjoyed the company since it made the time pass easier while I did the dishes. I don't remember exactly how I brought her up to my older brother, I didn't really think it was weird, but he informed me that her husband had killed her in the house, by throwing her down the basement stairs in a drunken rage. I knew I didn't feel comfortable going into the basement, but I didn't know why. I think I became a little afraid at that point, and started to shut out a lot of my abilities. I believe the spirit felt it as well, because I never saw her again after that.

I have been very close with my oldest sister for a number of years; she is ten years older than me, but we have always had a strong connection. She was actually my Matron of Honor at my first wedding. We had such a psychic connection going on, that we sometimes would call each other back and forth for hours on the phone, and not connecting, because we kept both trying to call at the same time! When one decided to stop and let the other call, it was the same thing, we were now both waiting! As comical as it sounds, it was sometimes very frustrating! Most of my siblings are gifted as well, but to different degrees. Some of my siblings have drug and alcohol issues, which happens a lot to people that can't handle their abilities, and a couple of them chose to keep their abilities at bay, but pay close attention to their intuition for their own good.

As much as my psychic abilities of knowing things in advance was always very good, I shut out most of my mediumship abilities. Almost to the point of forgetting that they ever happened! Every now and then people would sneak through though. Whenever someone I knew died, they would come to me immediately and tell me they were dead. That included my grandmother when she passed, and people I only knew as acquaintances. When my second husband's father passed away, a few years prior to us getting married, he came to me in the bathroom of the funeral parlor. He gave me a message, and asked me to give it to the family. I sat my soon to be husband down and explained that I needed to tell him something. I then explained what his dad did and said, and told him that he can't tell his family, because I was afraid they would think I was a freak. The first chance he got, he told his family. Needless to say, I felt uncomfortable around them for quite a while, although they never brought it up.

There came a time when I was overwhelmed in the businesses I was in, and going through a difficult divorce, and having an extremely difficult time getting over what I later found out was my "twin flame", and I went to see a medium myself. I didn't feel like I could trust my own intuition anymore, and felt like I was making decisions based on fear and desperation. She recommended I start meditating, and ask my guides on the other side to help me improve my intuition. I guess I didn't really understand at the time that my intuition was the same thing as my psychic ability. Be careful what you ask for! Apparently they had just been waiting for me to ask to open back up! They started coming through like I hung up an open for business sign! I started having random people that I didn't know coming through at all hours of the day and night!

I was working in my business at the time doing Aesthetic services, and putting my hands on the clients. Every person I touched brought a whole new flood of people and animals coming through! The first was a big white dog to jump in my lap! I asked the woman as discreetly as I could, that if I told her that I just saw a big white dog jump in my lap, would it mean anything to her? She got all excited, and said that she just put down her white Maltese the day before, and she was so happy to know that he was around. It continued from there. I asked her why she was so worried about her husband, and proceeded to tell me he was alone in Florida right now. I started getting an image of a house in my head that I described to her. I thought it was the house she lived in, but the angle I was getting looked like it was on the water, and she said it didn't sound like her house. When she was getting ready to leave, she ran over to me with her cell phone, to show me a picture her husband just sent her of the house I had described, and the caption read, "our new house in Florida"! This continued, with every person I got near. I was getting flooded with scenes of their life. One woman I asked if she had been cleaning out an attic recently. She confirmed that her aunt had passed and they had cleaned out her attic the weekend prior. I told her I was seeing a sock monkey, and wondered if she had found one. I thought the woman was going to pass out! She looked at me and said, "I found a sock monkey puppet in her attic".

The next woman, I described her entire living room for her, what the Christmas tree looked like, and where it was placed, what her daughter and husband looked like, what she had bought everyone for Christmas, and what her husband had gotten her and where he got it! She thought I had been in her house, and knew her husband and it was some kind of a joke! I thought she was kidding me, and just telling me yes to play along! That was it. I had definitely lost my mind! I needed to figure out how to make it stop! I started randomly calling every Psychic and Medium I could find listed online and asking for help!

A NIGHT ON THE OTHER SIDE

I was very lucky to have been directed by the other side to teachers that help me understand my abilities and how to turn them on and off. I ended up training for over a year, at places my mother who is also a medium, studied at over fifty years ago! My abilities grew very quickly, because I was apparently meant to do this work in this lifetime, and I've done it in many past lives. It took a while for me to come to terms with the abilities that I have been given, and understand that I have an important mission here on earth. Not only is it to learn and grow for my own soul, but also to help others heal the problems and heartache that they didn't heal with their loved ones before they passed to the other side. Yes there is another "side". I'm still amazed at what I see every day!

One of the most difficult things I have to go through, are the comments and remarks made by people who aren't yet awakened. I was never a very religious person, but I've always considered myself very spiritual. I have never tried to push my belief system onto anyone, and would expect the same respect from anyone else. Having seen what I've seen however, and knowing what I know, it's difficult for me to deny that it's real. More real than the everyday motions we go through here from day to day. There's absolutely no way I can deny that I'm conversing and seeing Angels and souls from the other side, because there is absolutely no way I could know the things that I know otherwise. Like many people, I sometimes have a hard time believing it myself! I then remember that I have to trust. It's all about trusting that what I'm doing is god's work. He gave me this gift for a reason, and directs me every day to the people that need me, and the people that teach me more each day!

I ALWAYS FELT LIKE I WOULD NEVER LIVE TO SEE 30

I noticed that most people that have been on the "other side" explain it similarly. A feeling of love and joy, so deep that it's hard to describe! Bright white lights, a deep feeling of unconditional love, and a feeling of being as light as a feather! It's all true! Your life also flashes before your eyes when you die. It's like a very quick review, but it's only the important moments you had, with the ones you loved.

I died when I was 27 years old. I knew I was going to die, and put my surgery off for five years because of my "knowing", until I had no choice. I had a "knowing" during those five years, that if I went in for the surgery I needed, I was going to die. Of course everyone, including my husband at the time, thought I was just scared, and that it was a normal reaction to having to have a serious surgery. The night before my surgery, when they were doing an MRI dye test, I died. I was twenty seven years old. I had a severe allergic reaction to the iodine in the dye. It was almost instantaneous. I saw the monitor flat line, and I was gone! It wasn't like falling asleep, but more like falling into a little bit of a mist when I left my body. It didn't hurt at all, in fact I felt nothing! I watched the scene from the top of the room, outside of my body. In the meantime, I heard voices, not just the ones in the room, and around the hospital, but coming from higher up above me. As I was reviewing my life, and thinking about my two children at the time, I was told that it wasn't supposed to be my time. I was flying, not floating! I could see not just my room; I could see all the rooms! I could see and hear what everyone was doing in the hospital! I was almost overwhelmed with the feeling of pure love and joy that just kept washing over me in waves! I was told I could stay if I wanted to, or I could go back, it was my choice. I now tried to bring my focus to my body lying on the table below. They had tipped it completely down, with my feet up, and the doctor was slapping my face, and yelling at me! "We can't lose you"! "We can't lose you"! I felt nothing, I wasn't in my body! I had seen him hit the big button on the wall when I first left my body, and a nurse came running in with a "crash cart". They were using shock -paddles on my body, and trying to get a heart- beat. They then injected something into the IV line. I thought about who was going to raise my children if I wasn't there. I thought about how much I loved them and still wanted to see them grow up. I decided to come back. It was almost instantaneous when I made the decision, I was back in my body.

When I came back, the Doctor told me I was very lucky. He was a Resident at the end of his month long training. He said if it had been the beginning of the month, he wouldn't have realized it wasn't a normal reaction, and I probably wouldn't have made it. I didn't bother telling him how close I came to staying on the other side! Our souls are all made of pure energy. Amazing energy!

Knowing the things that I know now, I laugh! They knew all along I was going to choose to come back. They know everything that's going to happen before it happens. They don't always tell us, so they don't influence our free will, but they know! I still had a lot of things left to do in my life, including having my youngest son.

My younger sister passed in December of 2011. She was the first of my siblings, (eight of us in total) to pass. Even before my parents. I still hadn't embraced my gifts yet, but she came to me the night after she died. Not only did she show me what happened, but we had a nice chat. I had been her legal guardian for many years, and she had a lot of animosity for me because of it. She and I have cleared the air, and she comes through more and more often as time goes by. I asked her when our dad was going to die, since he was already 87, and had been fighting cancer for years. She told me he was going to go in December. Of course when the next December rolled around, I was a basket case! I was telling my brother not to go on vacation, but I couldn't tell him why! I didn't want him to think I was crazy! He and I hadn't had a conversation about any of us having any gifts yet. Well December came and went and my father was fine. In fact, four more Decembers came and went, and he survived. On the fifth December, he had already taken a turn for the worst, but was stubborn and holding on as long as he possibly could. My brother thought for sure he'd make it to another Birthday in March. By then, I had embraced my gifts, and explained that our Sister said December when I asked her originally. Sure enough, he passed December 21, the first day of the Winter Solstice.

My sister also went to visit my mother after she passed. I was the one to tell my mother that she had died. She and my mother had never really reconnected, and didn't have a very close relationship. My mother didn't go to the funeral due to the distance and not being comfortable around my father. My mother said she had a message for me however, from my sister about a week after the funeral. My sister said to tell me that she loved the pearl necklace I let her borrow for the showing, and was happy I remembered what her favorite dress was. No one knew I had put my own pearls on my sister during the wake, especially my mom not being there. My brother had also picked a different dress out for the funeral, and I told him what her favorite dress was. It wasn't anywhere to be found. For the life of me I don't know how I found it back then, other than her leading me to it. It was still at the dry cleaners when she passed, and I had found it just in time for her to be buried in it.

LIFE ALWAYS WORKS OUT

Life is funny, you never know where things are going to lead you, but if you look back, everything you've done has taken you to the next step in your journey. It truly is a "journey"! The older you get, the more you realize that it goes so fast, and we spend so much time focusing on the things we want, or the things we want to be different, that we forget to look at where we are at any given moment. We don't appreciate what we have, and we stress over things we have no control over. The reality of it is; we don't really have control over anything in our life. We just want to think we do! Everything that happens in our life is meant to happen, and it happens for a reason. There are no accidents!

If you have children, you wouldn't have had those children with anyone else other than the person you had them with. So clearly, it was meant to be. If you think back over every event that's ever happened in your life, as difficult as it was, even a death, something good came out of it as a result. That's how life works. Not that you can't change your direction with your "free will", but sometimes it's nothing more than a detour on your journey.

Hopefully we learn some valuable tidbits of information as we go along our journey. If not, you'll see that you keep repeating the same things over and over until you learn. It could be picking the same type of partner; it could be having the same arguments and drama with someone until you get it. It's like life presents you door number one, two and three. If you keep choosing door one, and door three is really the one that's meant for you, the path will keep bringing you back in front of the same three doors, until you make the right choice, door three, and continue with you journey.

I feel I've lived many lives in the half century I've been on this earth. I also feel like my work has only just begun, and I'm living my best life ever, right now. It took me being able to be comfortable in the "who" I am, and embracing the gifts and knowledge that I have. I clearly cannot help everyone, and many people don't want help. I'm good with that! As long as I'm able to help the people that come to me, and give peace to both them, and their loved ones on the other side, I've served my purpose! It truly is an amazing feeling when you're able to connect people between the two dimensions, and give them closure or heal some wound.

Please understand all I do is interpret, and be the mouth piece. The real work is being done through me, not necessarily by me. My work is trying to interpret all the signs they give me, and try to hear all the words they're saying so quickly! That is where the real work comes in. The more souls I interact with, the more signs and symbols my Guides teach me, and the more detailed the messages.

WHAT EXACTLY IS A "MEDIUM"?

We live in a world, where people are beginning to realize, there are things that we don't all know, and maybe, just maybe all the Angels, Saints, and souls really do exist! Maybe we don't "know it all"! More and more people are beginning to awaken, and realize that everyone has some level of psychic abilities; they just need to want to tap into them, and expand their own abilities. Every Medium is a Psychic; every Psychic is not a Medium. Psychic information is information that comes to you from the other side, usually your guides but sometimes from the Angels. It's that feeling you get in the pit of your stomach when you know something is about to happen, or the voice in your head that tells you to go a different way to work today, and low and behold you avoided trouble of some sort! A Medium, talks directly to the people, or "souls" on the other side of the veil. Some can see them, and hear them, like myself, and some just get symbols. Like anything in life, some are stronger, and better than others.   You can learn how to develop your own skills. You may only be Psychic and not a Medium, but you can learn how to develop your skills with classes and practice.

Mediums, such as myself, can actually converse with the souls that have passed to the other side. Everyone's abilities are a little different. Some mediums are stronger because they were born with the gifts like I was. Most of us work very hard with the spirit world, to be able to interpret what they want to communicate. It's not usually a conversation, like you and I would have. It can be very difficult for some to connect between the two worlds. They vibrate at a very high frequency on the other side. Hence the reason when you see a "spirit", it's usually a quick glimpse. We as humans, vibrate much lower. Mediums vibrate at a higher frequency than most people. Therefore, I need to try and raise my vibration even higher, and the souls on the other side need to lower theirs, so we can connect. Then we get into how much energy the soul has that wants to come through. Very few souls have the energy to actually have a conversation. When they do, they talk so fast, I usually just let them talk through me, it's easier! Most will give you a word, a letter, and more often, a picture to get the message across. It's almost like a game of charades playing in our heads, and the medium has to try and interpret what the spirit is trying to say. This is where we need to spend a lot of time with our guides on the other side, so that they know what signs we understand. For instance, if they show me a picture of a beautiful woman like a vogue magazine cover, I know the woman really liked high fashion. (Most of the time)! And this is where things can get tricky, and a Medium can get the wrong message. If they showed me a white Buick, does that mean they loved that car, they sold Buicks, they had a car accident in one, or maybe they collected them? There are many possibilities. This is where we need input from the person that's receiving the message, so that we can now interpret the rest of the messages properly. It's not a fishing expedition, but we need confirmation, so we know we're on the right path with the message. To many people think it's like using a telephone and calling up a friend! It's a lot trickier than that to communicate!

I was never a very religious person. I grew up in a very broken home, and was exposed to many different religions. My mother sent us to attend many different churches. Presbyterian, Protestant, a Catholic School for a year, Episcopalian, two of my sisters were followers of Hare Krishna, and finally the Spiritualist church. I think my mother was searching, since unbeknownst to me, she is also a Medium!

I find it interesting, that although I didn't adhere to any particular religion, and still don't, I have always thought of myself as very spiritual and very connected to the other side. I was never really sure about Angels and Saints etc., but I know now they are very, real!

My parents separated when I was ten, and my father basically kidnapped the five youngest children that were still living at home. He told us for years that my mother threw us out, and didn't want us. He told us she was crazy! I didn't see my mother for about thirteen years. When we finally reconnected, I learned she was also a Medium. When I finally embraced my gift she was thrilled, and just by coincidence, did most of my studies at the same places my mother had studied more than fifty years before me! My oldest sister was the first person to really "out" me, after I put my mother in the nursing home at age 92. The nursing home called her, and wanted to put my mother on Psych medication, because she was telling people that she saw Spirits in her room, and would talk to them. My sister informed them that there was nothing wrong with our mother, she is a Medium, and that in fact I was also a Medium! I guess if I wasn't ready for the public to know, I'd better get ready!

I had a little bit of difficulty coming to terms with publicly being a Medium. I'm kind of a private person, and believe it or not, a huge skeptic! I've been to psychics, and Gypsys! I've heard the "give me $500 and I can fix whatever your problem is"! I think it's terrible! They have psychic ability, but that's it! Their motive is to know just enough to lead you on, and keep getting more money from you. They aren't Mediums, or healers. I don't believe that the Angels and Guides from the other side will work with you if you're not doing this work for the right reason. Hence the reason they don't have that ability. I may be wrong, but I haven't seen it yet. Even some of the "Public" mediums on television, are not doing this for the right reason. They're coming from ego, and are self-serving. For that reason, they will only be able to give very short messages, not detailed and not very accurate. Those people's abilities are very limited from the other side. They serve a purpose, as far as getting the public to realize that this is real, but their focus is not on healing. They are on their own journey however, and hopefully will learn that money and notoriety mean nothing. You can't take either with you on the other side. I can however take the memories of the people that I've helped get closure with their loved ones, and I'm sure I'll be greeted on the other side by the souls I help there.

I used to be a very black and white person. It was on or it was off. If I couldn't see hear feel or touch it, how could it exist. Even though I've been seeing spirits since I was a child, I had trouble grasping that it was an ability that I had. Just like the Universe. I could see the stars and the moon, but to fathom galaxies or theories I had difficulty with all of that. Like a lot of people, when odd things happened, for the most part, I tried to ignore it and find a logical explanation for it. When they were right in my face, like my father in law after he passed, I accepted it, locked it away and went on again with my daily life. I used to go to haunted locations for vacations, because I always seemed drawn to the other side, without really understanding the why behind it. I lived in many haunted houses, not realizing that most houses have spirits in them. The difference was, I could see and hear them, and they knew it! Unbeknownst to me, they were just waiting for me to be ready....

There came a time in my life, that I was having trouble with all the changes happening. I had gone through a long drawn out nasty divorce, and a breakup with what I later discovered was my twin flame. For the first time in my life, I couldn't get a guy out of my head, or my heart. I also didn't trust my own intuition on the decisions I was making on a daily basis. I started to see a medium as a healer, and she recommended that I try meditation. I started to meditate, and asked for my intuition to become stronger. Little did I know at the time, that intuition IS your psychic ability! Well that's all they had been waiting to hear on the other side! They started coming through like a floodgate! I had all kinds of animals, and people coming to me like crazy! Anyone that I was with, I could now tell you everything about that person! What their home looked like, their spouse and children, what was going on in their life, it was just insane! I also didn't know how to turn it off! I went to bed at night, and I was surrounded again! Just like when I was a child! I was getting woken up at all hours of the night, and could see them going in and out of my bedroom. Needless to say, this was not what I was expecting!

Fortunately, there are other people out there like me, who had been working and dealing with this for years, and the Spirits directed me to them for knowledge. The first thing I needed to know was, how do I turn it on and off? You can't possibly live this way! You would never get any sleep, or get anything done! I was being woken up all night long by people coming to me for help that were lost, people that I knew that had passed, people I didn't know, and I didn't have any boundaries. I spent a full year training and practicing how to turn it on and off, how to talk to my guides, and learning symbols and signs from the other side, before I tried to help anyone on this side. Then they started bringing people to me. I noticed that every person the Spirits brought to me, allowed me to help them, while teaching me something else about the other side. There is always more and more to learn from them, and they continue to accommodate!

My Gatekeeper is the Guide that keeps the souls at bay for me on the other side. He also lines them up one by one for me when I'm doing an audience. I've only actually seen him once, and he has only spoken to me twice. He's an American Indian ancestor of mine. He and I have an agreement. No one can come through if I'm not "working", unless it's an emergency. Every now and then someone sneaks by that's not actually an emergency, but it's a rare occasion, usually because I got interrupted, and didn't close down!

THE HIERARCHY OF THE "OTHER SIDE"

I believe we have one god, or higher power. Not necessarily a male or female, but a higher Spirit, that you can give any name you want to. They are made of pure love and light. We also have Angels on the other side. Angels were never people. They are their own race of beings, and their only job on the other side, is to help and work with us. There are millions of Angels on the other side. They have their own order as well. We know about the Choir Angels, the ones that sit the closest to god. The first Angel I ever channeled, while I was doing a Reiki session on a woman, was a choir Angel. She filled the room that I was in with bright golden white light. She was so large I could barely see her wings! I ended up down on my knees with tears in my eyes, because the love that I felt was just so overwhelming. She had come to tell me that she was protecting the woman and her child, because her child was meant to be very important when he grew up, in regards to helping humanity. All I heard was Seraphim when I asked her what her name was. When I was done with the session, I googled the word, to find out she was one of the ten highest of choir Angels. It was such an amazing experience; it's stayed with me like it was yesterday. Under The Choir Angels, you have the Arch Angels. We know many of them, like Michael, Gabriel, Ezekiel, etc. Then we have the regular Angels that just hang around us all day long to help! The rule with Angels however, is that you have to ask them to help you, otherwise they can't intervene. Their rule, not mine! I don't usually ask the why behind things, I accept them as I learn them.

Then we have our Guardian Angel. Our Guardian Angel is actually not an Angel at all. When we're born, one of our family members on the other side either offers to be your Guardian Angel or someone from the group is elected to do the job. We all have one. They're there all the time to help guide us. If you're going down an icy road, and lose control of your car, and swear that someone else was steering you to safety that would be your Guardian Angel. They don't have to wait to help you if they feel it's an emergency. They try to give you hints, and place people and things that you need in your path, but they're also very careful not to change your journey. If you need help with something, you can always ask them, and they'll be there. Your Guardian Angel can change. If for instance, you have a dear friend, or a relative that you were very close with, and they pass, they can ask on the other side to become your Guardian Angel. In those instances, the original Guardian Angel steps back, oversees the situation, and only steps in if asked to specifically.

And lest we forget some of the most powerful allies on the other side, the Ascended Masters! We all know some, but there are so many it's hard to know them all! Jesus is probably the most well-known, however there are many more. Mother Mary, Mary Magdalene, St. Germaine, Buddha, Confucius, and the list goes on and on! They were all once human, and walked the earth. They are fully enlightened, and have decided to work as teachers and protectors for us all on the other side. Again, all you need to do is ask for help from them, and they are more than happy to oblige!

Then there are just regular guides that you can call upon any time you need to. They're people that lived and worked on earth, and have offered to give their help to guide us and help us as needed. For instance, if you were trying to write a book, you would ask to channel the guide that can help you the best. You don't need to know their names; they'll just come through and help. I have clients that have high profile jobs, and still call on their professor s from college to help guide them in a project they're working on, and people that ask to channel people that were mentors in their life to give information that's pertinent. They are very happy to help if we ask.

THE WAR BETWEEN GOOD AND EVIL

I truly believe there is a war going on between heaven and hell to claim souls. Keep in mind, where this good there is also evil. Everything in life is a balance. Black balances white, night and day, up and down, Ying and yang, it goes on and on. Most people don't see the difference between good and evil, because they are so caught up in their daily drama. If they don't have drama they create it, to take their focus off of what's really important in life. The more pure of heart you are, light workers as we're called, the more of a target you are for evil. Each side is trying to claim your soul for their side. This is the reason it's so important to ask for protection before you open yourself up to meditation, each and every time. It's easy for people to get an evil attachment, depending on their lifestyle. The lower vibrational entities like to gather in places like bars, and crowded venues. If you're drinking too much, you're an easy target for them to attach to you, because you don't have full control of your senses. Anyone who is an empath, or an extremely sensitive person, is more vulnerable to being attacked or attached to. An Empath is someone who absorbs other people's feelings when they are around them. They feel what you feel. Most light workers are empaths. It can be difficult for empaths to go out into crowded situations, because they can easily become overwhelmed. It's also important if you are an empath, to clear those feelings you've absorbed every day, so they don't affect your personality. A salt bath or shower will work. You can also sage yourself. Daily relaxation rituals can help as well, like relaxing with chamomile tea. They should avoid stimulants like caffeine and alcohol as much as possible.

Evil likes to feed on negative energy. If you have an attachment, the first thing it will try to do, is to cause havoc in your home. It will change your mood, so that you become angry or argue at any little thing. You may find yourself drinking more, or using other drugs as an escape. It all opens you up more for them to get inside, and possess your body. This is what evil entities want to do. They want to be in a body again. The angrier you get, the more you fight, the more energy you build, and the stronger you make it! Many people have no idea they've been "taken over", but the people that love them will notice the personality change. Catholic Priests are doing so many exorcisms, that they actually started giving some classes to non-priests to help them with the onslaught of evil!

The best way to protect you is to always choose the honest and honorable choice. Be truthful, caring and loving. Make a close connection to god, the Angels, and your Guides, through meditation and prayer. Wear religious medals, or a cross. Have some type of religious ornaments in your home, whether it's a statue, a cross, or a picture on the wall. Evil is visual. It sees and feels. If it sees these things around you, and feels the light around you, it will stay away! I promise, for those of you who sit on the fence, and aren't really sure, once you pass to the other side, I guarantee you'll be a believer! In the meantime, you having everything to gain, and nothing to lose but your soul!

HOW DO I CONNECT TO THE OTHER SIDE?

This is a wonderful question, how to I connect to the other side? Mostly through meditation! It's something that everyone should learn and connect for themselves. Once you've mastered the art of meditation, you'll find that you can actually connect to the other side very quickly. You also connect to the other side every time you step into nature, by really appreciating what you see. Being grateful is another way that we connect to everyone over there as well. Most people never express their appreciation for the things they have in their life, or the accomplishments they've made. We never do anything in this lifetime alone. There are always many people on the other side that are working very diligently to orchestrate events in our lives. Whether it's a lesson we need to learn, or a person we're supposed to meet, and have no knowledge of, or if we've prayed and asked for something directly, they all have a hand in it. Acknowledge them and the results. Be grateful and thank them for all their hard work. Everyone, no matter here or there wants to be appreciated and recognized.

How do you begin to meditate? It needs to become part of your regular routine. Something you do at least once a day, if not more. There are so many benefits to meditation. It's been proven to lower your blood pressure, help with anxiety, lower your cortisol and stress levels; help with migraines and depression. It's amazingly beneficial! You can start out slowly, and try to increase both your time and your frequency. There are many wonderful meditation cd's and apps available for phones. I recommend starting out with a guided meditation first, then when you're comfortable, you won't want or need it. Oprah Winfrey and Deepak Chopra have a wonderful guided meditation that you can listen to for free on their website. They also offer a 21 day free meditation two to three times per year. You can also go to YouTube and listen to many different meditations. Find a comfortable place that you can try and be in the same place and time every day. Make sure you are sitting upright, preferably with your feet on the floor to stay grounded. I always recommend that my students protect themselves before starting any type of meditation. Whenever you open yourself up to the other side, you open yourself up for evil to get in just as much as the Angels. There really is a war of souls going on here, and evil tries to sneak in whenever you're not protected. I ask for Arch Angel Michael to surround me with love and light, and protect me from any lower vibrational entities, any attachments, and from any harm. While I'm asking, I also ask for him to protect my loved ones and my loved ones loved ones as well! Never pass up an opportunity to ask for protection for evil, it's everywhere! You then want to try and picture tree roots growing out of your feet. Picture them going down into the earth very deep, and anchoring you so you don't float away! Meditation will take you out of your head, and literally off the planet! If you don't stay grounded properly, you can walk around with a spaced out feeling in your head, not thinking clearly when you're done. This can last a long time! For this reason, many light workers end up overweight, because they end up eating after meditation to feel more grounded. Take three nice deep breathes, in through your nose, and out through your mouth. You want to make sure they are deep enough to see your diaphragm expand, not shallow breathing, Oxygen feeds your brain. If you start breathing very shallow, you won't get enough oxygen to the brain, and you'll lose the connection to the other side. I then ask for my Guides, the Angels, the Ascended Masters and Arch Angels, and any other higher vibrational entities that are around, to come into my aura and be with me. I ask them to give me messages and information that are clear, concise, verifiable, and for my highest and best. If there is something specific I want information about, I ask, thereby setting my intentions. Then you try to clear your mind. If you start to think about something, try to let it go, and picture it going right out of your head. Try and look for the pinpoint of light that you see. Picture it getting larger and larger, and filling up your whole body, going straight to your heart center. You may see faces as you meditate, or hear voices, as they are trying to connect with you. You may also feel like someone is touching your hair, your arm, or another part of your body. Sometimes you might smell something out of the ordinary, like cigarette smoke if the person coming to you was someone who used to smoke. Feel free to have a conversation with whomever you want to connect with. You may just get words in your head as an answer if you're asking specific questions, or have a memory or sign just pop into your head. This is how they communicate on the other side, mostly with signs and telepathy. If you're asking for them to help you do something on this side, pay attention to the signs and signals they send you on this side. Lots of sequential numbers, like 444, 1111, tell you that you're on the right path, and connecting! Of course there are technical terms for what you're hearing, feeling or seeing; I'll list them briefly without going in to too much depth, because I think they're pretty self-explanatory. Clairvoyance is the gift of seeing things, Clairaudience the gift of hearing things, clairsentience, the gift of feeling something, and Clairgustance, the gift of smelling something. Last but not least, Clair cognizance the gift of knowing.

You can also connect by just sitting in the power, and connecting with "god", or whatever other name you're comfortable with. This just recharges your batteries, and gives you amazing energy! Just get comfortable just like you are going to meditate, but ask to connect with the Great Spirit, or the God of Love and Light, and say that you just want to sit in the power. You want to just feel the love and light flow through your body. I usually do this a few times a day, for anywhere from ten to thirty minutes. You may find that you slip into a meditative state, that's fine, just bring yourself back to sitting in the power. When you're finished either meditating or just sitting in the power, it's extremely important that you thank everyone that came through or gave you information, and close down the session. If not, it's like keeping your windows open in your house all the time, anyone can come in! If you're walking around in an open state, you can still have messages, or spirits coming to you.

It's an amazing "gift" that we all have the ability to connect to the other side.

WAYS TO KEEP YOUR VIBRATIONS HIGH

The number one way to keep your vibration high is to meditate, and be grateful for the things you have in your life. Besides meditation, you can just sit in the "power" of god, and feel his love and light recharging you! Always stay positive, and look for the good in any given situation. We all have a down day here and there, but shake it off as quickly as you can! Get outside in nature; enjoy the little things life has to offer, like the smell of the rain, or the sound of birds chirping. Listen to children laughing and playing. Listening to music also helps to keep your vibration high. It doesn't matter what genre you like, as long as it's uplifting you. Make sure you're eating properly and getting an adequate amount of sleep and exercise. Remember that life is all about balance, so make sure you have that balance between your work and your home life. Going out in the fresh air and sunlight, and wearing bright colors also helps.

There are many different types of crystals that you can wear or carry that can help keep your vibrations high. Any of the crystals in the quartz family vibrate at a high level, and can keep you vibrating higher. Rose quartz can help keep you heart centered with your thoughts and citrine quartz can help you to attract money into your life. Amethyst is also pretty to wear and vibrates very high. If you want to study crystals, there are crystals to help with any problem you're having. Selenite can absorb negativity, I carry it around in my pocket, and tiger eye can help you with your clairvoyance! There are many books out there that you can get. To clean your crystals, and get the negative energy out of them, you can soak them overnight in a sea salt bath. (With the exception of selenite, it cleans itself, and you don't want to get it wet).You can also put them outside on a full moon to clean and recharge them.

Spend time with the people you love, but stay away from drama. Find your passion in life, and follow it. You may love to paint or cook, or just entertain friends. Maybe you're a reader, or someone who likes to travel. Whatever it is that truly makes you happy, will raise your vibration. Just do it!

SIGNS THAT THEY ARE TRYING TO CONNECT WITH YOU

When you're asking for things of your angels or Guides, whether it's to help you get a certain job, to help you or a loved one, or even to locate something you lost, they will try to give you signs that not only did they hear you, but they're working on it from the other side.

One of the first things you may see is repeating numbers. It could be 1111, which is a sign that the Angels are working on your issue, 555, that a big change is going to be coming to your life soon, a license plate with a word, or initials on it that you would recognize, or many other types of thigs. Animals running in front of your car, or seeing something that's out of the ordinary is always a message. One deer crossing your path would mean something totally different than having several cross in front of you. You can either get a book about signs, or you can google what the Spiritual meaning of the sign may be. Signs can mean different things depending on the person. Many of the signs will tell you many different meanings when you go to research them. Always chose the one that resonates with you. Some are just obvious! For instance, you may see a license plate that says "Angel" or your mom's name if she has passed and is trying to contact you.

Keep in mind, that although they hear you, and as long as what you asked for is for the highest and best of all concerned, that it can still take some time for it to come to fruition. There is such a thing as divine timing. Be assured however, they will continue to give you signs that they're working on it, and it will happen eventually! It all has to coincide with your soul's path in life. You need to be awake and aware enough to recognize the signs, so you can stay on the right path.

I was waiting for my Twin Flame to come back into my life for a very long time. I understood the reason it was taking the time it took, was that he still needed to awaken, and had something that he needed to learn. I also needed to understand that my life's lessons were to have faith and patience. I received a message that they he might be returning sometime around spring time, or the time of the daffodils blooming. (Knowing that they have no sense of time on the other side, and it had already been over three years, I was skeptical about the timing again). It was a cold late spring, and the first time I saw daffodils, I was excited, but thought to myself, maybe they bought them at Easter and just planted them, since no one else had daffodils. I then drove to the gym the next morning, and saw a yard full of daffodils. Still no sign of him coming forward, I still doubted the confirmations they were trying to give me from the other side. Three weeks later, I went to visit one of the Newport Mansions, and went outside to enjoy the gardens. They had a three acre area, covered in nothing but daffodils. That still wasn't enough for them on the other side; they wanted to pound the point home. The entire ride home, all of the road medians were covered in Daffodils! They still weren't done. I got on the highway, and just thought to glance to my right for some reason, and what did I see? A giant heart made of daffodils on a hill on the side of the highway! Yes, I got the message! They're still working on it for me, and it will happen. Needless to say, although they are giving me signs that they're working on it, for whatever reason, my Twin Flame isn't ready yet. Probably a slow learner! Three weeks later, while driving my car, I see a truck with 1111 on the license plate. The next day, I see a license plate with his initials and birthdate on it. They still aren't done reassuring me, two days later on my way to a doctor's appointment, a car cuts in front of me, with MRSROB on the license plate! I'm thinking to myself, really? What are the odds? They have to be astronomical! They still weren't done though! That night on the nightly news, on a station I never watch, they showed a brief clip of him on the news. He has a high profile job, and every once in a blue moon is in the news. The Angels are basically telling me that they are still working on it, and it's going to happen! They really want to help and reassure us from the other side. We have to be awakened and aware to see the signs they're sending us, to keep us on the path be belong on. Sometimes it's like a trail of bread crumbs, or a dangling carrot!

They'll also try and connect with you through your dream state. We here on Earth are in what's called "3D". Your dreams are in "4D". The Angel's and our loved ones are in "5D". That's also where your "higher self" resides, the part of your soul that is outside your body. One of the easiest ways they can connect with us, is through our "4D' state when we are sleeping. You'll know it's a connection, and not just a dream, because it happens right before you wake up, and you'll remember it. It feels different than a dream. I always recommend having a pad and paper near your bed, for those moments that someone does contact you, and you wake up. If you don't write it down right away, you will start to forget everything they had to tell you.

MY THOUGHTS ON REINCARNATION

Understand that there are no accidents in life. Everything that happened happens for a reason. If it's not for you to learn, then you're helping someone else. We all have free will, but the reality is, if something is meant to be, it will be. We always have some responsibility for the things in our life, but the reality of it is, we are only delaying the inevitable most of the time. If for instance, you were meant to be with a certain person in your life, you may separate for a period of time, because one or both have a lesson they need to learn, but you will come back into each other's lives at a later time. It you were meant to take door number three, and you keep choosing door one, your journey will keep bringing you back to the same choices, until you decide to take door number three. Just like the person that keeps getting into the same type of abusive relationship. They will keep offering you a different choice, until you are ready to take it. Then you can continue on the path you were meant to be on. All you did was keep detouring and delaying the inevitable.

The only two exceptions I have been able to find to this are when people pass outside of their time. Suicide is never written into our life plan. Someone that commits suicide has let everyone down. It's like they just quit the game of life, and now everyone has to hustle to come up with other options for the people still here. If you die in an accident, and it's not really your time, they don't get stuck, but they do take longer to adjust on the other side because of it. Usually it's due to a decision they made, not someone else. I've found that people seem to reincarnate no sooner than every three or four hundred years. They seem to like to wait until everyone that remembers them plus a few generations have passed until they come back again. There are exceptions it seems to everything though. Of all the hundreds of people I have brought through to loved ones from the other side, I have to date, only had one little girl from 1980 that I was unable to bring through. Her brother had come to see me, and wanted to know more than anything who had murdered her. After several attempts to contact her, and not being able to find her, relatives came through to tell me she was not there, and that she had reincarnated almost immediately. They also wanted to put his mind to rest, and let him know that the person that murdered her had been arrested for another murder, and had either died or been killed in prison.

I've also been asked why we don't reincarnate as aliens. Maybe we do, I don't know! I have only channeled one Alien, who is a guide for me. He guards the Akashic record room, and helps me do research. I've never asked him about it. I have however channeled him to answer questions for people that have been abducted multiple times, to explain the reasons behind it. I believe we probably reincarnate as what we are the most comfortable. Cleary for most of us, that's human. Maybe if you have alien DNA you can choose to try out an alien body some time! I'm sure at some point they will educate me further in regards to this and many more questions that arise, and I will pass on the information when I receive it.

When we're ready to reincarnate, we get together with the people in our soul group, and make a plan. Almost like creating a board game. Our Soul group, are the people that we reincarnate with each lifetime. You meet with a "committee" from that soul group to see if you are ready to come back, or if you created so much bad karma to clear in the last lifetime, that you need to work on it a little more there first. My understanding is that all the Arch Angels head up the soul groups. I am in Arch Angel Michaels Soul group.

Therefore, if you are my life in any way, you are in that soul group as well. I know we can interact with people from other soul groups, but I haven't spent enough time researching this with them, to find out if we can cross to another, or how much interaction there is between groups, etc.

The only thing that is not written into anyone's plan is suicide. We do write exits in sometimes, if our life has been extremely difficult, and we can take that exit if we want, just like when I died and chose to return. Suicide however, is tantamount to quitting the game. When we do this, we leave everyone that we reincarnated with hanging. Everyone that we were supposed to touch or interact with now has to have a new plan. Our higher self, (the part of our soul outside of our body), works with the Angels to help fix the journey for anyone impacted by the suicide. Once they get to the other side, most of the people that committed suicide are extremely remorseful. They see from the other side the impact they made by letting everyone down. They need to spend time working on the cause, so that they can enjoy the other side, and not repeat it when they come back. They also need to try and minimize the negative Karma it created.

Our souls are very large. They're too large to squish everything into the body we live in. This is why you see an aura. That's part of your soul that doesn't fit, also known as your higher self. Your soul is all knowing. When the time is right, it trickles information to you that you need to know in any given situation. For example, you may have a partner that's cheating on you. Maybe it's in your soul plan to have a child with this person. If you found out too early, that might not happen the way it's supposed to. Therefore, your higher self won't give you the information and clues for you to learn about the information until after the baby is either conceived or born. Life is all about timing.

Can we reincarnate as animals or trees? Again, I don't really know the answer to the question about trees, because I really haven't delved into it too much. I do however believe that we can. I know we can reincarnate as an animal if we so chose. I inherited a dog from one of my children, who was not able to keep the dog after having a baby. Her name is Dulce. Dulce was just too nervous around the new baby. My son felt very connected to the dog, as did I, and was heartbroken to have to give her away. I'm glad I was able to take her. She seems to have "people" eyes, and acts more like a person than a dog! She sleeps on a pillow while she watches television on the couch, and reprimands my other dog when she misbehaves! She's extremely overprotective of us, and always wants to hug like a human. I asked about her when I was in my Akashic records, and was told that we had saved her life in a previous lifetime. In that lifetime, she had been a man. She came back as a dog, and was specifically meant to protect us as a way of repaying her debt. (Karma) So yes, I do believe that we can come back as an animal, but I still don't know about plants and trees!

READING THE AKASHIC RECORDS

The Akashic Records are your "book of Life". Everyone has one, and almost every religion speaks of putting your name in the book when you're born. It's a complete history of every lifetime you've lived. It includes who you were, who was in your life at the time, including the people in your life at this time, and everything you did or happened to you in that lifetime. The main purpose of the record's, is to be able to clear Karmic things, and problems that you're having in this lifetime. If for instance, every man you marry dies in this lifetime, as was the case with one of my clients, we can look back on your past lifetimes and determine the reason why, and what lesson it is your supposed to be learning in this lifetime. I've learned that we reincarnate with the same group of people each lifetime, and many of the same people appear in each lifetime, however not always the same position that they were the last lifetime. For instance, your son in this lifetime may have been your father in a past life. Your neighbor may have been your brother or your boss in a past lifetime. They show up here again, so that you can either repay a debt, or collect a debt from a past life, or learn something from them, or teach each other something. I've found that there are many different groups that reincarnate together. Each Arch Angel is in charge of a different soul group. I am in Arch Angel Michaels soul group. There for, most all the people I run into, because we are interacting in this lifetime, are all in Michael's soul group as well.

The first time I got into the Akashic Records, it was by accident; it's said that if you end up there, or are somehow drawn to the records, than you are meant to be a reader. Apparently there aren't that many people who read the records. I was in a guided meditation class, and we were doing astral projection. My soul ended up not only leaving my body, but leaving the planet! I was in this very large hall, and I could see a room off to my left, and lots of bright white with walls that see to go up forever. There was someone standing at a podium to my right that I directed my attention to. He wasn't human; he was very tall, and blue. His body was cylinder shaped with heavy blue robes, and his hands were tucked inside by his side. I didn't look up into his face, he was very tall. I wasn't afraid, but definitely felt intimidated and nervous. I asked him where I was. He told me I was in the hall of knowledge. He said it was where everyone on the other side could go and learn what they wanted to know, He said all the knowledge of all the Universes was held there. I then got a little excited, and said "this is great"! "I'm all about learning and knowledge"! I asked if he could show me around, and he obliged. He took me into an area that looked like a spiral hole, filled with books going all the way around and all the way down. Across from it, I could see almost like a large screen in an IMAX theater, with things being displayed in nature. He then proceeded to have a book float up and handed it to me. He escorted me to the room I had seen on my left when I came in. He proceeded to explain that this was my book of life, and told me I could look at it if I wanted to. I opened the book, and it was like it became alive! The book started to display like a three "D" movie all around the room. It was really amazing. I wasn't looking at things to come; the book doesn't show you that, but things that had happened in my life when I was a child. I watched for a little bit, and then brought it back to him in the front of the hall. I thanked him, and still not looking all the way up into his face, asked his name. He told me his name, which I had trouble pronouncing. He laughed, and told me I could call him "grey man". I said, "but you're blue not grey". He laughed again, and said "that's ok". After years of learning different things, I believe it was an inside joke on his part. He is a Palladian, from the Palladian Galaxy. They are apparently here to help us on earth. The "greys" as they're called, are a race of grey aliens that don't like humans. They are the ones abducting people and experimenting on them. I'm sure he knew I'd get the joke eventually!

Every time you are reincarnated, you come back with the same soul group of people. Everything that ever happened in your life is in your book. No one can read your "book", without your permission. No one can read anyone's book if they are under the age of 18, because the knowledge could alter their life, and they may not be ready to process the information. There are rules to follow just like everything else, for many reasons. You also cannot access the books if you've had any mind altering substance for twenty four hours prior to reading them.

If you're having a problem in this life, whether it's with a person, and something else, by going back in the records, you can heal the problem in this lifetime. I myself have been afraid of deep water since about the age of 10 years old. It was like a switch was flipped, and I could not go in water that was over my head. I tried everything, including scuba lessons trying to overcome the panic I would feel, but couldn't clear my mask to pass!

I knew I had drowned in my passed life, but had no idea how. When studying the records, I found my answer! In my very last lifetime, I was an herbalist that lived on the outskirts of a small village in Europe. When someone was sick in the village, they would come to me to make an elixir for them to get well. I've always had an affinity for mushrooms as well. I love to eat them, and always wanted to go mushrooming, but even with the books I have to identify them, I've been reluctant to go search for them. There was a sick girl in the village, about 10 years old. (The same age as when it affected me in this lifetime). She had become ill, and they asked me to make her an elixir. Unfortunately, I made it with poison mushrooms! Needless to say, the little girl died. My punishment was to tie rocks to my body, and throw me into the river, where I drowned.

After finding out the information, and going through it, seeing my spirit leave my body, I was over it! I went for lunch that day, not even making the connection, and bought three bathing suits! Without even trying them on! (They did all fit perfectly)! Since that time I've been snorkeling, and don't feel so panicked in the water.
This is just one example of many things that can happen when you go into your records.

HOW DO THEY LOOK WHEN I SEE THEM ON THE OTHER SIDE?

When souls pass, they are still the same people over there that they were here. If you dad was a miserable bastard here, he's going to be a miserable bastard over there too! They don't miraculously turn into a new person! Many times they will see things from a different perspective, and realize that they made mistakes here, and wish they had done things differently, but not always. Sometimes they are stubborn or in denial about how they were when they were here. Some souls will work on themselves on the other side to become more enlightened, and not repeat things when they come back, and others seem to not really want to learn, and not really care. They are all different. It can be a major challenge when I bring message through from them, because I don't always know if they are being completely honest with me either! I've brought through Priests that were pedophiles, they still deny that it happened, and child molesters that still blame the victim, or say that it never happened. It's their reality, and their perspective, and that's what we need to know on this side. You may or may not hear what you want to hear.

For the most part, souls will come through to me either the way they looked prior to passing, so I can describe a specific ailment and the sitter can recognize them, or the way they thought they looked the best in this lifetime. They always are coming from their perspective however. For instance, I had someone's mom come through, and I described her perfectly, including the fact that she was a successful Real Estate Agent. I mentioned however that she showing herself a little overweight with her glittery outfit. The family immediately wanted to discount all of the evidence I had given them that it was their mother, because she was showing herself to me overweight. They then remembered, in life, their mom had an eating disorder. She was extremely thin, because in her mind she was always overweight! This is why you need to keep an open mind, and remember that it's their perspective, their show, and their message. I have another woman who was a blond for about a month in her life. Her family hated the color, and she quickly changed back to brown. She apparently loved the blond hair however, and comes through as a blond every time!

When talking to them on the other side, you also can't have expectations. What you feel is important is not necessarily important to them on the other side. You may want to hear them tell you something specific that's important to you, but they're going to talk about what's important to them. Many times people are looking for apologies that aren't always coming. I also have yet to have someone tell me where the buried treasure is, although I did have one tell me where the key to the safe deposit box was! Most of the time they're concerned with things like family recipes, traditions, letting loved ones know that they're spending time around children and grandchildren. If they are on the other side with a spouse or partner, if they were a loving couple here, they are still a loving couple there, and usually come in together to show me. If they were not prone to public displays of affection, they will just stand next to each other, possibly with an arm around each other. If they were always showing affection here, then they do so as well there, so that I feel the love between them.

WHAT'S IT LIKE FOR THEM ON THE OTHER SIDE?

After you pass, you also lose the ability to enjoy things the same way you did when you were here. You can't smell food, or taste food. You can't feel someone's soft skin or enjoy having sex. I believe these are some of the reasons we chose to come back and reincarnate again. Almost like reincarnating is a vacation from heaven, as loving and lovely as it is. They mostly have to live vicariously through us from the other side after passing. There used to be an old custom; that you should set an extra plate at the dinner table for someone that recently passed, so they could join you for dinner. I love this idea, because that's exactly what they do! They love to be remembered and thought of, and when they have an opportunity to speak to you from the other side through a medium such as myself, most can't wait! No one wants to be forgotten, they want to be remembered, and they want you to know they're around you very often. They still see your struggles, they share in your grief and your sorrows, and they're still trying to help from the other side. For them, it's like they're standing behind a two way mirror. They can see you, hear you, they can even touch you, but you can't see them, and usually don't understand that the sensation you're feeling is them. I'm sure it can be very frustrating for them at times. This is why they try to leave you signs that they're around. They have the ability on the other side, to go anywhere they want, and do anything they want to do. Many times they will come through to tell me that they're visiting places they always wanted to go to when they were here, or that they spend their time in a place they loved visiting when they were here, like Paris. They don't spend all of their time around people they know that passed; in fact, every now and then I have one asking about someone that also passed, because they apparently hadn't looked for them themselves on the other side. Although they do know everything that's happened here, and everything that is going to happen, I guess sometimes they just don't apply themselves! They can look anyway they want, and they can do anything they want over there. It seems like they spend a lot of time enjoying things, and people here. Many grandparents still tell me they're here watching and playing with grandchildren. They can come and go from the light at will. If we call them, they show up almost immediately, even though you can't see them. At some point in time, most decide it's time to learn. Although they learn soul lessons faster here than on the other side, eventually I believe they all do some soul work over there. The more work they do there, the less lessons they have to learn when they come back here. Not that the lessons are any less difficult for older souls, just possible less of them.

What can you do on this side to help them on the other side? The biggest thing you can do is be happy in your life, and remember them. If you're stuck in grief here from losing them, and you stopped enjoying life, they're stuck with you. When they see you cry; they're sad. They have no body there, they can't taste food, they can't smell perfume, and they can't enjoy pleasures like sex. They want to live vicariously through your happiness. When you're enjoying life, and you're happy, they're happy. Remembering them with stories to other people, and celebrating customs that they shared, like recipes that they passed on, makes them very happy. They're all about love and family on the other side. Family is not just who you marry or are born to, we are all each other's family.

WHAT KINDS OF SIGNS
DO THEY SEND US?

They are always trying to give us signs so we know that our loved ones are around us. You might smell their favorite perfume, or cigar or cigarette smoke. You may find object left for you or something you left somewhere moved. They love to do the disappearing reappearing trick! Anything that they think will get your attention to give you a message that they are around you. They can also manipulate nature. You may find a white feather, to know the Angels are near. You may have a stray turkey, deer, or other animal cross your path at an unusual place or time. You may see a flower bloom outside of the normal time. They're clever with change as well! You may find pennies or other change in places you normally don't, or everywhere! They might direct you to a place where you'll find something that was a special memory to you or them. Repeating numbers are a big one, but those are mostly from your Angels. You need to be aware, and then look for the meaning they're trying to convey to you. There are books you can buy, as well as sites you can google. Things mean different things to different people, so always go with the meaning that resonates the most for you. Some souls seem to have more energy than others. I don't really believe it has much to do with how long they've been on the other side. I've had people that just passed come through with a lot of energy, and some that have been on the other side for quite a while that have very little energy. It does however take a lot of energy for them to teleport an object, or move a heavy object like a door. They seem to get a kick out of making noises, like footstep sounds. They can draw energy from things on this side to help them to communicate or move objects. That's why you may get your batteries drained, or your light bulbs dim a little when they're in the area. It explains why the lower vibrational entities, i.e. ghosts, can seem to slam doors and throw things very easily. They're drawing a lot of negative energy by causing anger and fear, and feeding off of that. Souls that come back and forth don't do that.

They're always very grateful to the person coming to me for a message, and to me as well, for giving the message to them. It's sad that so many people refuse to open their minds and hearts to let them in, usually due to some outdated scare tactics that many religions try to instill. I promise, when everyone gets to the other side, you'll realize how foolish you were!

IS THERE A HELL?

I absolutely believe there is a hell. I haven't seen it, I really don't want to. I have however chased demons and very evil spirits around homes, and removed them as attachments from people. They aren't from heaven, so they had to come from someplace else! Many people are under the impression that hell is here on earth. I think that nothing could be farther from the truth! I believe this is meant to be like a playground for us, although many of us forget that when we get stuck in the drama of life. Earth is like a middle ground, and when you are awakened, you'll see the beauty in everything and everyone. I believe that everything in the universe has to be in balance. There for, knowing there is a heaven, it stands to reason there must be a hell. I also believe that anyone that takes a life with ill intention goes to hell. This would basically be a murderer, but not someone that accidently killed someone, or killed them in self- defense. Believe it or not, I haven't found any other people not in heaven. I've channeled some pretty mean and nasty people, from people trying to get answers and closure, and they are still in heaven. God truly is a forgiving god!

I also believe that there are layers of different dimensions, in heaven here, and in hell. This is where it gets a little complicated, because the past, present and future are all happening at once in any one of these dimensions. Then there are layers, like a cake! Depending upon your belief system, that's what helps to determine the layer of the dimension that you end up going to. That way all the people with similar beliefs are interacting together. The Hubble telescope took a beautiful picture of ice in the universe. It looks like an ice castle. That's the best description or picture I've seen yet, as to how to describe what it looks like. This is a topic better saved for another book!

THERE ARE SPIRITS EVERYWHERE

There are a lot of souls that are just plain "stuck" here for different reasons. I always try and move souls into the light if I encounter them here on earth. Many of them are here because it's a safe and comfortable place for them, and they don't know what's in the light. They just stay, in the same era that they died in on the other side. I have encountered many attics and basements full of immigrants that came to this country illegally.

I once chased a demon around a three family apartment building in New Haven Connecticut. The family had a demon attached to two of the family members, and they had moved nine times in less than seven years. The basement of the house was full of the souls of illegal Irish immigrants that came over during the potato famine. The Demon had told them they couldn't leave, and that they would burn if they went into the light. They were in the house prior to the demon arriving, but he was now feeding off of their fear. The attic was full of Italian Immigrants, in the same situation. In all of these instances, these were safe hiding places for them when they were here. Thus, when they passed, they went back one by one to what they knew. I moved all of these people into the light. When Demons come in contact with me, they run. They know that I am pure of heart and intentions, and I come from the light. Nothing scares evil more. The souls also see the white light emanating from me, and know what I tell them is true. After assuring them that their loved ones are in the light waiting for them, they go. I was asked to tour a mansion in Newport a few years ago. When I got to the attic, it was full of black slaves that were stuck there from the Underground Railroad days. Unfortunately it was the first time I had come across a situation like this, and I was so overwhelmed I didn't think to try and cross them into the light. I'm not in contact with the people that are in charge of the facility, but since they also do ghost tours there, I'm under the impression they would not allow me back if I told them my intention would be to cross them over.

I've also come in contact with lots of souls stuck because they don't really understand they're dead. Believe it or not, every hospital, funeral parlor, nursing home, and cemetery is filled with souls that don't realize that they're dead. A lot of times they follow the body after they leave it. If they start to wander around, and someone now moves the body, they have no idea where it went and hang around hoping it's coming back! There are lots of souls roaming the streets, and hitchhiking in cars etc. It would be truly frightening if everyone could see what it looks like! I've also crossed over people that didn't live a good life here, they were alcoholics and drug addicts, and they're afraid to go into the light and confront their loved ones because they know they caused them pain. I assure them their loved ones have forgiven them, and sometimes call them from the light to have them escort them. Then there are the ones that are here because they enjoy what they're doing and don't want to go into the light. I've seen women cooking in kitchens for families that are long gone, because they just loved cooking and enjoyed what they did! It's almost like they're in their own little time warp! Usually when I tell them that their family is in the light and they don't need to be doing things here, they go. Occasionally I'll have someone who's still working or doing something they enjoyed here, and refuse to go into the light. If they stay though, it has to be with an agreement that they don't bother the families or co-workers. These entities are of a lower vibration than the ones that are in the light. Some of them can be dangerous, if they want to attach to you, and live through you. I always recommend everyone have religious statues, crosses, things that are religious symbols on their body and in their home as a deterrent. These souls are not the same as the souls that are living in the light. When you relatives come visit you from the light, as they can come and go as they please, they aren't stuck. They vibrate at a very high rate of speed, and have a very light feeling about them. The lower vibrational stuck souls feel very heavy to me, because they vibrate slower.

MANIFESTING WHAT YOU WANT IN YOUR LIFE

The Universe is made up entirely of energy. We are all made up of energy, as are the souls on the other side. Energy cannot be destroyed, but can change. It also flows. Thoughts are energy. Just as the saying goes, "you are what you think", you can also manifest what you think. Where you thoughts go, your energy flows! Energy spins like a huge vortex. If you look at a tornado, that's what pure energy is like. In order to manifest the things you want in your life, you need to be part of the vortex. How do you get into the vortex you wonder? By asking, being grateful, meditating, being positive, and appreciating the things that come to you every day through your Angels and guides. It's all about a positive attitude, and maintaining focus on the positive things in your life and in the world. By practicing these things on a daily basis, and paying attention to the opportunities that are brought to you, you will get into the vortex!

Pay attention to the cycles of the moon and the planets. Everyone and everything is affected by the gravitational (energy) pull as they move around in the skies. Set your intentions on the new moon every month, and write down in a journal the top ten things that you want to manifest in your life.

Every full moon, write them down again, and take them outside to burn them under the full moon, and send the wishes up to the universe. Believe it or not, it works! Energy goes where your thoughts flow! It may take a few months, but you'll see results. The more you work on manifesting, and the more grateful you are for the things in your life, the faster things will come!

Clear out any bad energy or spirits that may be in your living or working space. This is done easiest by burning sage. It also offers protection from any negative or evil entities. While burning the sage, with a window open for the negativity to leave through, go from room to room starting either attic down or basement up, and ask the Arch Angel Michael to remove any negativity, and allow only love and light to stay. Make sure to get behind doors and under beds, negative entities like to hide when they see you coming! You'll feel the change in the energy right away. Always try and do this on a regular basis, and after having any company that could have brought some negativity with them. You can also leave small dishes of holy water near the entrances to your space. This is great for a work environment where many people come and go. The holy water will absorb the negativity, and actually keep out anyone that's truly evil! You'll notice some dishes evaporate faster than others in the same room, depending on how much negative energy it's absorbing. You can find crystals that help keep your vibration high, and can help attract positive things that you want to manifest. Carry some with you, and keep others in your space. Connect with nature as much as possible. God created this beauty for you to enjoy it! When you connect with nature, you're raising your vibration, and helping to stay in the vortex. Lead a healthy lifestyle. It's hard to be in the vortex if you're impaired by drugs and alcohol, or if you're polluting your body with cigarette smoke. Your body is your temple. You only get one, you chose it, take care if it!

Behave like you already have what you want, and it will come. For instance, if you want a job, get out of bed at the time you normally would. Dress as you would for the job. Discipline yourself to look and apply for the job you want, and believe that you're going to obtain it. Eventually, you will!

Don't live in "lack". If you focus on what you don't have, you'll end up always wanting, and having less. If you focus on what you do have, and be grateful, it will multiply, and the universe will continue to bring you more.

If you want more money in your life, you need to have an attitude that you already have money, and you'll always have money. How do you do that? With a "nest egg"! That's why they call it that! Save an amount of money that you're comfortable with, either five or ten thousand dollars. This is money that you're NOT going to spend! It's just "there"! Watch how quickly your attitude about money changes, and how much more money will start to arrive. It's all about intention, and energy! That's how you manifest!

SOME OF MY ACTUAL READINGS AND MESSAGES

HELP! I THINK HE'S CHEATING!

I had a woman come to me who was having problems in her marriage. She thought her husband might even be cheating on her, and she didn't know what to do!

With the Destiny Card Program, (The cards of the Magi) I was able to confirm that first, her and her husband were Twin Flames. She had no idea what that was, but once explained, was able to verify as well. (They even have a daughter who was born a two of hearts, a twin flame herself, of a twin flame couple)!

By going through her husband's cards, I was able to decipher that he was stressing out over a change in work, and contemplating some new things on the job front. He was also having a mini mid-life crisis! The cards also confirmed that the sex level had really dropped off, and he was missing the intimate moments they used to have. The cards show that he was starting to communicate outside the marriage, either looking for advice or comfort, but hadn't strayed, and wasn't likely to. They were definitely meant to be together for the long haul!

By going through the cards, we were able to come up with a plan of action, to not only to help her put her marriage back on track, but her own career as well! She followed my advice, and her husband to this day keeps thanking me!

* * *

THIS IS WHY WE DON'T DRINK & DRIVE!

There's nothing more heartbreaking than bringing through children that have passed to talk to their grieving parents.

I was volunteering my services at one of the churches, and two weeks in a row I had parents come to see me that had lost teen age children in car accidents. The first one was a young girl about 17 years old; that was in the back seat of a car being driven by someone that was impaired. She knew she shouldn't have gotten in the car, and although her parents always told her to call them if she needed a ride, she didn't. She came through very upset, and thought her parents were angry with her for getting into the car with a drunk driver, against their teachings. The parents couldn't believe she thought they would be mad at her, they loved her so much, and they were just stuck in grief due to missing her!

She did let them know that it was a very quick passing; she actually jumped out of her body upon impact. She didn't suffer. That's what every parent wants to know when they lose a child. She was relieved on the other side, to know that they weren't blaming her, even though she knew it was her own fault for getting in the car. As difficult and heart wrenching as it was, they were all able to get closure and heal.

The next week the Aunt of one of the other teenagers in the same car accident came to see me. She had no idea that the other parents had come to see me the previous week. Her niece was also a passenger in the car, it had hit a tree. There were four teenagers in the car at the time, and they all perished. She was hanging around for the most part with the girl I had brought through and talked to the previous week. The woman actually came to see me more for the girl's mother's sake, since she was having a difficult time with her passing, and felt that she was still in the home. We were able to confirm that she was in fact spending all of her time with her grieving mother still in the house, and had been trying to make her presence known. I was able to give her information that hopefully will let them move on, and allow her to heal on the other side as well.

During this Holiday Season, it's my hope that we all remember that our actions effect many people.
Please be safe on the roads, don't drink and drive, and don't get in a car with an impaired driver.

PEOPLE DON'T CHANGE WHEN THEY PASS!

I had a girl come to see me that wanted to have some closure with her Father, who had passed many years ago. She is in her mid-50, and her father had molested her as a child. She wanted to know if he was sorry for what he did, and how it had affected her life.

The first person that came through was a man in farmer jeans. that kind of looked for lack of any better description, like a farmer. She was very excited to talk to him, and recognized him right away! He was a neighbor when she was growing up, that was more like an Uncle to her, and had always watched out for her as she got older. He basically said he came in to protect her from her father, since she was calling him in to talk to him.

The next person I saw was this guy that felt like a shady character, kind of creeping up on us. He was on the shorter side, and looking all over the place, like he was watching his own back. She confirmed that it was definitely her father! Sadly, until a soul is ready to work on the things he did outside of his life plan, and become a better soul, they stay stuck in what they did and who they were when they were here. I could tell he was not a nice individual.

She asked him why, she wanted an explanation, and wanted to know if he was sorry. He first denied that he did anything wrong, and then tried to blame everyone else! First it was her mother's fault, because he didn't really want to have kids. He then tried to lie his way out of it, claiming he was just a hard working guy, and the reality was that he spent his time and money in the bars. He then blamed the girl herself, because she was to "pretty" for him to resist!

She was able to get closure however. She was able to tell him what she thought of him, and that he's not a part of her family anymore.

It seems to be a common theme of molesters on the other side. Another girl that came to me with the same problem had a similar response from her father. Her father however was rude and using foul language as he blamed her for his actions! He was so nasty, I had to send him on his way, but not before she got her say, and told him not to be anywhere around her when it's her time to pass!

Every soul is different, just as every person is different while they're here. Some start working on themselves right away, and enjoy the freedom they have on the other side, others stay stuck and it takes them much longer to work on themselves.

* * *

Every Day I'm amazed!

I never know what situation I'm going to have when I do a reading for someone. I recently had a woman come see me that wanted to talk to a friend that had passed away. He was coming through to me loud and clear, a very strong spirit. He informed me that they were much more than friends, and that he had bought her an engagement ring. She admitted that they were a couple, but didn't know about the ring. I then asked him to tell me how he died. He said it was very quick, and it was just a bright light through his body, and his heart stopped. He relayed it similar to being struck by lightning! I wasn't getting anything clear from him. I asked the friend how he died, and she informed me it was a suicide. I then got information that he had hung himself in his bedroom closet, but do to the fact that he was heavily medicated on prescription drugs, he had no idea that he had been responsible for is own death! He heard her tell me it was a suicide, and he was quite surprised! He then became very remorseful that he had done this, and caused her so much pain. He almost seemed lost prior to being told that he had killed himself, but after knowing this, felt relieved to know, and able to process the whole situation much better. It's always very fulfilling when there is help and closure on both sides of the veil!

* * *

The Spirits in the "tree" souls never want to be forgotten!

A while back a friend came to see me. He was concerned about another friend, who seemed obsessed with a tree that he drives by every day near his house. He was pulled so much to this tree, that he would just sit near it in his car for hours, and started to take branches home that had fallen off onto the ground. He was starting to act like a different person. He was having trouble sleeping, and couldn't think of anything else but the tree.

One look at a picture of the tree, and I knew right away it had been a "hanging tree"! I could picture the poor families from the area, women and children, lined up and hung one by one in the branches. This was done by the Indians in the area at the time of the great Indian wars. I could see and feel the anguish of the men they loved finding them there, and taking them down. There was so much sorrow.

The tree held on to this sorrow. I believe that many of the people were even buried close to the base of the tree. Some of the souls were trapped inside of the tree, since it seemed like a safe and nurturing place for them. The sadness however still overwhelmed the tree and the area.

I believe that the man taking the branches was reincarnated from the time period, and his family was some of the people hung there. I immediately instructed him to return the branches he had taken, since it was the same as taking something from a grave. He returned the branches, and started to feel better, but still wanted to know more about the people and the connection. He visited the local historian to try and confirm what I had felt.

Within a few months, he was driving by the tree, and saw that it had fallen down. The parks people were removing it. The entire inside of the tree was hollowed out, the space where all the souls were residing. He had a sense of sadness, and at the same time a sense of relief upon seeing this. I believe that once the souls were recognized, and their horror remembered, they realized it was time to be released and move on into the light. No one ever wants to be forgotten. They want to be remembered

NOT A SUICIDE

After I started to really embrace my gifts, I began offering my services for a nominal fee at charity events. I was still trying to perfect my skills, and learn from the other side! When something like this happens to you, it's normal to ask. "Why"? What's the reason this happened to me? What am I supposed to do with this "gift"? (That sometimes feels like a curse)! Well I got my answer on New Year's Eve a few years ago.

I was doing a charity event in Newport. It was my second time doing the event, and I guess word had gotten out about my abilities, and that not only am I authentic, but truly gifted. After having done some 30 readings back to back all afternoon and ready to call it a day, a woman came over and asked me if I was finished. I said that I was. She then asked me if I would mind seeing her mother, since she had been waiting for me to be done with everyone else before seeing me. I looked over to my right, to see a woman in her early eighties sitting at a side table. I noticed them earlier, and they had been waiting over an hour. I agreed to do one last reading. The daughter sat at the table behind us, so her mother could have some privacy.

The woman brought her mom over, who seemed a little bit frail, and quite anxious. I asked her if she would like a general reading, or if she wanted to talk to someone on the other side. She blurted out very quickly, that she wanted to talk to her son. I said o.k, but would you like to talk to your parents first, since your dad has been standing next to you the whole time you were here? Sure she said. When I work I ask for people to tell me yes, no, or I don't know. Unless I ask a specific question, I don't want them leading me somewhere with "my" thoughts that I don't want to go. I offered to describe who I saw, and she could confirm whether or not she recognized them. I asked her if he used to have a car with a hand crank on front to start, because that was what I was being shown. She did not know. I then asked if dad would have some occasion to be wearing a tuxedo with a large top hat, long tails, and a small cane used as a prop. Absolutely she screamed! That's my dad! Then a woman came into the picture, wearing a long ball gown, with a tiny waist and a mink stole. Yes, she confirmed, that's my mom! I have the same picture hanging over my fireplace! After they said the "I love you's", dad made mention that he was disappointed that the family bloodline ended with her. (She had no sons), and because her brother had no children, which she confirmed.

She then again asked to see her son. I had her call his name out loud three times, which seems to help them come. I then described the man that came next. No she said, that's not my son, it's my brother! I asked her if she knew her brother had been murdered. She confirmed that she did, and the killer was caught. He wanted to thank her for taking care of him growing up, apparently there was a huge age gap, and their parents were socialites that were never home. He also wanted to tell her how sorry he was that she had so many tragedies to handle in her life, and wanted her to know he was always with her. He then went on to tell her that he had two illegitimate children, in response to his father's remarks about having no bloodline. He informed her who the mother of one of the children was, but asked that she not contact them for their own privacy.

She again asked to talk to her son. I had her call him again, nothing. I then asked her brother to see if he could locate him for us. I saw him go back into the crowd of relatives, grab this person by the arm, and literally drag him up to the front of the crowd. As he stood there, his head was down, and he would not look at me. I explained to his mother, that usually means he is ashamed of something, and the fact that he didn't come on his own, usually means they had some kind of falling out prior to his passing. "I know why" she says! Please do not tell me I asked, only yes, no, or I don't know. I then asked "Do you believe he committed suicide"? Yes she yelled yes, I caused him to kill himself! At that moment, her son lifted his head, and very defiantly stated "NO, I did not kill myself! It was an accident"! His mom started crying uncontrollably! His sister came from the other table, "I knew it" she said. The police kept saying it was a suicide, but there was no note, he left dinner cooking, all the lights were on in the apartment, and he was doing so good with his new girlfriend!

I then asked him to tell me what happened. He said that they had changed his medication, which his mother confirmed. He said he had been watching this cool thing on television about this guy juggling a chain saw. He then just kept telling me how stupid he was, and how sorry he was. I then told his mother I felt something with his neck, but I didn't feel like it was a hanging. She then confirmed for me what he was showing me, that he dismembered himself. He tried juggling the chain saw and it slipped.

After we were done, and she was able to stop crying, I gave her a huge hug. She said she had lived the last 35 years thinking she caused her son to kill himself, because she was too tough on him! She had asked for him to come to her dreams, and nothing. I explained that he didn't know what to say, or how to approach her, because he felt so much guilt on the other side, knowing that he had caused her so much pain. I told her he should start coming to her in her dreams now, since they are now both at peace. I asked her, why in 35 years she hadn't gone to see a medium to get some closure. She told me she's been going to see them for years, and no one had been powerful enough to bring him through. I was shocked, and honored all at the same time. I now knew, that I was supposed to be doing what I'm doing, no matter what anyone says! If someone had been able to bring her son through years ago, she would have lived a very different life than the one she did, believing she caused her son's death.

AUNT, MOTHER, AUNT, WHICH IS IT!

I was doing a show on Cape Cod one evening. It was a corporate fundraiser for a nonprofit group. Four girls came over together, and asked if I could do an Angel card reading in regards to the new Real Estate business they had just all opened together. I agreed since they were all in the business together.

As I started the reading, there was a woman in a long white nightgown standing behind one of the girls. I asked if it was o.k. to see who she was, and what she wanted. I kept hearing that she was someone's mom, but then that she was one of the girl's Aunts! I was thoroughly confused as to who this woman was, until one girl said, "oh my god, that's my aunt, and her mother! We're cousins"!

The woman was showing me a scene from the hospital bed when she was dying, with everyone standing around her in the room as they made the decision to pull the plug. I could see her daughter, as a little girl, burying her head in someone else's arms, so she didn't have to look.

She confirmed that she was seven when mom died, and that she had been in a coma from an accident. Her dad had insisted she be in the room when they gave the last rights, and pulled the plug. She said she was traumatized from it happening that way, and really felt like she never had the opportunity to say goodbye.

Her mom was now showing me the girls' bedroom, with her picture in the upper right hand corner of the girls make up mirror, and wanted her to know she's with her every day. The girl started balling her eyes out, and confirmed that she does in fact have a Polaroid picture of her mom on the upper right hand corner of the makeup mirror. She was able to talk to her mom through me, and able to get the closure she couldn't as a child.

If there is someone you need or want to have closer with, know that it's always possible.

* * *

DON'T RATTLE THE MEDIUM!!

When someone wants to really talk to someone from the other side, they really should make a point to be open and cooperative, and not rattle the medium! We're people just like you, and we're not only using a lot of our energy to contact your loved ones, but we're also trying to hear them and interpret the signs and symbols they give us. They operate on a much higher vibration than we do as human beings, and it takes a combination of many things to get the message from them to you.

That being said, one of the worst instances I ever had, was an Italian woman at one of my shows. She wanted to talk to her mother who had passed, and was getting very annoyed when I brought in her Aunt, an old friend, and another relative, but not her mother right away. She started to get loud with me, and was tapping her fingers and swinging her leg back and forth while she was snapping her gum! We don't have control over who does and does not want to come through and talk to you! It's like a two way mirror, if they know you, or are around you and the facilitator, (me) is there, whoever wants to talk or see you shows up! In my experience, the people that don't come through for me right away, either had a falling out prior to passing, or did something shameful prior to passing. I have had 100% success rate however on bringing everyone asked for through, with the exception of one soul who had reincarnated shortly after her murder.

Finally her mother showed up! She was showing herself in a house coat in the girls kitchen, and told me her daughter would come for coffee every morning, which she confirmed. She also showed me an oxygen tank she was using to breathe, but wanted her daughter to know she wasn't smoking! Her daughter confirmed, she was on oxygen, and every time she saw her she told her she wasn't smoking, although she was. Her mom went on to tell me that she was more than a daughter, she was her best friend, and they spent every weekend going out shopping together and just having fun together.

Her mother wanted to know why her daughter wasn't wearing a necklace that was very special. The daughter informed me that she had given her mother the necklace, and had been wearing it, but thought it was too big to wear all the time. Her mom then apologized to me for giving me such a hard time bringing her through, but she thought her daughter was "mad" at her, since she wasn't wearing the necklace! We need to keep in mind; it's their show, and their perspective!

It's almost funny, that we never know what they're thinking on the other side, but they're always happy to hear from us!

WHY ARE MY EVENTS DIFFERENT?

What I've discovered from doing my events is that most people go to a Gallery Reading of Mediumship, hoping to talk to someone specific. They have an expectation, and when someone different comes through for them, even though they received a message, they feel disappointed! The shows that I've attended, the Medium will speak to whoever comes through, and then hope someone claims them!

It does happen that I have souls sneak through now and again and need to determine who they are, why they are there, and what their message is, but for the most part, I prefer to bring through the exact person you want to talk to. Most Mediums apparently are not able to do this very often; I so far, have been able to bring through everyone that I've asked for. Sometimes another relative will come through first, because they can, lol, and usually have a message or want recognition. Sometimes the Soul I'm trying to bring through may be upset with the person asking for them, which makes them a little more stubborn about coming through, but inevitably, I've been able to coax them!

 All in all, I recommend everyone have an open mind when attending an
event, because even if you don't receive a reading, or have someone come
through, many times the message that comes through is meant for more than
one person. They do try and be efficient when they can! I hope you check out
my event schedule, and if you're too far away or unable to attend, you can
always book a private session in person, by phone, or by skype.

* * *

ALWAYS KEEP AN OPEN MIND WHEN TRYING TO CONNECT WITH YOUR LOVED ONES!

Always try and keep an open mind when trying to connect with your loved ones on the other side. Many times Souls on the other side come through to the Medium the way they looked before they passed on, or the way they thought they looked the best in this lifetime. I have one woman who always comes through as a blond, although she was blond for only about a month during her lifetime. Her family hated it, but she loved it! Immediately however, the sitter thought it was not the person he wanted to connect to because of the blond hair. I was able to give him details I would never have known, to confirm who she was.

I recently had another Soul come through very different at one of my last shows. The woman was coming through and trying to make the point to me that she loved things that glittered. She also saw herself living out some fantasy from an old Bogart movie, which was her favorite. She was however, coming through heavy set to me, not thin as she was in this lifetime, we finally figured out, it was because she always saw herself as overweight, and had an eating disorder.

Her family saw her as she was, very thin. She however, even in the afterlife, saw herself as overweight. You need to listen to what they are saying from the other side, and remember, you may not know everything about them that you thought you did! They run the show, and the message they give is what's important to them, not necessarily something important to you. They may not being telling you what you want to hear, but they feel the message they're giving is important. I can't stress enough, that when they are coming through to you, they show themselves from their perspective. The way they thought they looked, or the way they felt. You may think you know how they felt, but you may be wrong. The message they are sending is important to them, it may not be as important to you, or what you wanted to hear, but it's important none the less. What's even more important is that they're communicating with you. Listen!

DO YOU REALLY NEED TO WAIT A "YEAR" BEFORE CONTACTING SOMEONE WHO PASSED?

Do you really need to wait a "year" before contacting someone who passed? Absolutely NOT!! I recently read a thread from one of the "famous" television mediums, (that I won't name), who was telling people that they need to wait a year before contacting someone, because they're weak from passing, and it takes them that long to rebuild their energy! That is absolutely NOT TRUE! If a Medium is unable to bring a soul through, regardless of the time since passing, it's the Medium that's weak!

Regardless of when a soul passes, some are stronger than others. The weaker Souls tend to give more symbols that need to be interpreted than words for some reason. That's up to the Medium to work with their Guides to be able to interpret. Every Soul is different; however I've seen them so strong after passing that I need to get out of the way and let them just talk through me! A perfect example of this was an 80 year old woman I met, who had been going to Mediums for over 30 years, and no one was able to bring her son through until she found me! He was reluctant to come through, since he had caused his mother considerable pain, she in fact thought she caused his death, and it really destroyed her life. After having him come through, the situation was resolved for both him and her!

When a Medium tells you the Soul is on vacation, busy, not strong enough to come through, or just not around, it's not the Soul, it's the Medium. It can even be a challenge for me, if I'm having an "off" day, but so far, I've been able to bring through 100%, whether they died last week, or ten years ago!

As a matter of fact, everyone I know personally that has passed, has made a point of coming to me immediately after passing, (just to let me know), and I have yet to go to a funeral that didn't have the deceased standing watch with their loved ones, and sometimes enjoying the show!

THE SPIRITS DIRECT ME TO INFORMATION I NEED

I love how Spirit directs me to the information that I need when I need it. I recently did a large Gallery reading, and although everyone seemed very happy that received messages, I did receive a couple of emails that I truly took to heart. What I do is not easy work. It takes a lot of energy, and can be physically and emotionally draining. One audience member was upset that they didn't get a reading, although all shows clearly state that everyone won't. There just isn't enough time, and I try to do as many as possible.

They also didn't seem to understand how Mediumship works, although I do try to explain before I start giving readings.

It's not an exact science. For the most part, depending on the energy of the spirit coming through, I'm given images and pieces of words. I now have to determine what the meaning is. If for example they're showing me a car, I'm not "fishing" when I ask the meaning! Did they drive that kind of car, did they sell cars, were they hit by a car, is someone else driving their car? Unless the person I'm reading for can give me some clarity, I have no idea what they're trying to give me, and it makes it more difficult to connect the next images or symbols they're giving me. No Medium can be 100%

accurate; because it is based on interpretation of the symbols we're shown. Most of what I receive is symbols and images very quickly that I need to interpret. Very few Spirits are strong enough to give me lots of words, and when they do, I pretty much let them speak through me, because the come so fast!

I also give too much sometimes, which I was told through another email makes me inaccurate! Again it's interpretation. I saw a woman with a large beautiful hat, posing like she was on the cover of vogue. To me it represented that she was really into fashion, which was confirmed by the daughter. Another audience member however, took it literally that her mother would wear big hats, and stated that I was wrong!

Spirit directed me to one of John Edward's (no relation) books, (One Last Time), where I read how he actually sees and interprets messages. I thought somehow I was missing something. We see things the same way. He has just as much difficulty interpreting some symbols as I do! He has many more years of experience, but for the most part, we connect in the same manner. The more I do, the better I get at interpreting, just as he did.

They'll always be people that want to pick you apart, and be negative, they come to every show. I have to remember, I do this work for the people that need it, and are healed on this side and the other side of the veil, as well, and I will continue to learn what they want me to know from the other side.

Contact information for June Edward "The Massachusetts Medium"
Email
june@juneedward.com
Website
Juneedward.com
Twitter @junemassmedium
Instagram juneedwardmassmedium
Pinterest juneedward.com
Facebook JuneEdward11
Skype june@juneedward.com
Phone
508-259-1231

I offer classes in Psychic development and Mediumship twice a year currently, and hope to be adding more classes soon. Unfortunately they are only in person in Massachusetts, and not on the internet at his time.

ISBN: 978-0-692-15548-6
Imprint: Independently published

94490268R00044

Made in the USA
Lexington, KY
30 July 2018